Almond Flour Recipes

Homemade Breads, Snacks and Sweets

Contents

Almond Flour Recipes 1

About the Book 4

Introduction 5

Bread Loaves and Muffins 6

Date and Walnut Bread 6

Pumpkin Spice Bread 6

Banana, Pumpkin Layer Bread 8

Banana Bread Sampler 9

Zucchini Bread 10

Breakfast Bread 11

Apple Cinnamon Bread with Cranberries 12

Coffee Cake with Walnuts 13

Pina Colada Bread 14

Flaxseed Bread 15

Irish Bread 16

Banana and Blueberry Muffins 17

Peach Muffins 18

Zucchini Muffins 19

Greek Yogurt Muffins 20

Peanut Butter Muffins 21

Snacks 22

Multi Nut & Seed Crackers 22

Graham Crackers 23

Fig Crackers 24

Peanut Butter Granola Bars 25

Cranberry Chocolate Power Bars 26

White Chocolate and Macadamia Nut Bars 27

Almond Joy Bars 28

Nacho Cheese Bread 29

Cranberry Biscotti 30

Desserts 31

Apple Crisp Crumble 31

Peach Crisp 32

Chocolate Covered Butter Cookies 33

Honey Butter Cookies 34

PB & J Cookies 35

Peanut Butter Cookies 36

Pumpkin Pie Bars 37

Coconut Pie Bars 38

Mocha Latte Bars 39

About the Book

This is a guide book for creating delicious baked goods using almond flour. You will find 3 sections in the book starting with a variety of delicious flavored bread loaves and muffins. Following those recipes, you will find granola bars, crackers and breads in the snacks section. The last section will satisfy your sweet tooth with fruit crisps, cookies and sweet bars. Enjoy all the bakery style recipes with the added health benefits of almond flour.

Introduction

This book is written to help people take advantage of the benefits almond flour has to offer. What is the reason behind substituting almond flour where our typical wheat flour is? The almonds provide high protein, content, low carbohydrates and low sugars which is helpful in maintaining a stable glycemic index. It is easy to cook with almond flour because it is moist, unlike many other flour substitutes. Research has shown that replacing other carbohydrates with almond flour showed a reduction in the occurrence of heart disease and cholesterol.

Still enjoy your favorite, delicious recipes while giving your digestive system a rest from the inflammation caused by wheat. You will also benefit from nutritional contents of protein, magnesium and potassium. Not only that, the flour is easy to bake with and has a great taste. Try out these recipes and enjoy delicious baked goods with even more to offer,

Bread Loaves and Muffins

Date and Walnut Bread

½ c. sifted almond flour

2 tbsp. sifted coconut flour

⅛tsp. sea salt

¼ tsp. of baking soda

3 large dates, pits removed

3 whisked eggs

1 tbsp. vinegar (apple cider)

½ c. chopped walnuts

Heat up the oven to 350 degrees and grease a pan with coconut oil. Combine flours, baking soda and salt in a medium mixing bowl. Add the potted dates into the food processor gradually and pulse until paste like. Add in the flour mixture, then eggs, then vinegar. Lastly, add the walnuts and mix, careful not to make them too fine. Pour into pan and bake for 30 minutes.

Pumpkin Spice Bread

1 c. sifted almond flour

1/4 c. sifted coconut flour

2 tsp. cinnamon

1/2 tsp. cloves (ground)

1/2 tsp. nutmeg

1 tsp. of baking soda

1/2 tsp. of baking powder

4 large eggs

1/4 c. maple syrup

1 c. organic pumpkin puree

1 tbsp. melted butter

1 tsp. vanilla extract

Heat up the oven to 375 degrees and use coconut oil to cover the inside of a loaf pan. In a medium bowl sift together the flours, cinnamon, cloves, nutmeg, baking soda and of baking powder. In a separate bowl whisk the eggs and mix with syrup, pumpkin, butter and vanilla. Combine the two together and transfer to the loaf pan. Bake 40 minutes.

Banana, Pumpkin Layer Bread

1 c. almond butter

2 tbsp. almond flour

1 c. dried coconut (not sweetened and shredded)

2 bananas

2 large eggs

1 tsp. of baking powder

1 tsp. of baking soda

1/4 c. organic pureed pumpkin

3 tbsp. cocoa powder (not sweetened)

1 tbsp. raw honey

Heat up the oven to 350 degrees and grease a loaf pan. In a mixing bowl, mix the butter, coconut, bananas, of baking powder, flour and baking soda until smooth. In another bowl mix the honey, pumpkin and cocoa powder until smooth. Pour the banana mixture into the dish and spread evenly. Then pour the pumpkin in a layer over the banana. Bake 35 minutes.

Banana Bread Sampler

6 overly ripe bananas

4 dates, pits removed and dried

4 large whisked eggs

⅓c. coconut cream

3 tbsp. almond flour

2 tsp. pure vanilla extract

¼ tsp. of baking soda

¼ tsp. of baking powder

1-2 tsp. cinnamon

Pinch of salt

Sliced banana

Chocolate chips to taste

Dried fruits

Heat up the oven to 350, grease 3 mini pans for loaves. Puree the pitted dates until the consistency forms a paste. Then add in the bananas, eggs and butter. Once those are smooth, mix in the remaining ingredients and pulse until smooth. Divide between 3 mini loaf pans. Top one with sliced bananas, stir the chocolate chips into the second, and mix dried fruit into the third. Bake 45 minutes.

Zucchini Bread

½ c. almond flour

1 c. zucchini (drained and grated)

3 large whisked eggs

1 mashed banana

Pinch. of baking soda

3 tbsp. melted honey

1 tsp. ground cinnamon

½ tsp. salt

1 tbsp. melted coconut oil

Heat the oven to 350 and grease a pan for loaves. In a mixing bowl, combine flour, cinnamon, baking soda and salt. In another bowl whisk the eggs, melted honey, mashed banana and oil together into a smooth consistency. Add the grated zucchini into the egg mixture and disperse evenly. Stir the flour mixture into the egg bowl until thoroughly combined and without lumps. Pour into the loaf pan and bake 30 minutes.

Breakfast Bread

½ c. almond butter

2 tbsp. almond flour

2 large whisked eggs

2 tbsp. raw honey

1 tsp. vanilla extract

¼ tsp. stevia

¼ tsp. salt

¼ tsp. of baking soda

1 tbsp. ground cinnamon

Heat up the oven 325 degrees and grease a pan for loaves. Use a food processor, hand mixer or by hand to blend the almond butter until it becomes very creamy. Once it is, whisk in the flour, eggs, stevia, honey and vanilla until smooth. Stir the salt, cinnamon and baking soda in and incorporate well. Bake 15 minutes.

Apple Cinnamon Bread with Cranberries

1 ¼ c. sifted almond flour

½ c. sifted coconut flour

¼ c. ground flax seed

½ tsp. sea salt

1 ½ tsp. of baking soda

1 tsp. cinnamon

½ c. pecans (chopped)

3 whisked eggs

¼ c. melted coconut oil

½ c. unsweetened coconut milk

¼ c. maple syrup

1 tbsp. vinegar (apple cider)

1 c. chopped apple

½ c. dried cranberries

Heat up your oven to 325 degrees and grease a pan for loaves. (Coconut oil works great) Mix together the cinnamon, flours, flax seeds, salt, chopped pecans and baking soda until well combined. In another bowl whisk the eggs and mix them with oil, syrup, vinegar and milk. Pour the egg mixture into the flour bowl and beat on high for about 5 minutes until well incorporated. Add in the chopped apples and cranberries and distribute throughout. Pour into the loaf pan. Bake 45 minutes.

Coffee Cake with Walnuts

½ c. sifted almond flour

1/3 c. sifted coconut flour

½ c. melted coconut oil

½ c. coconut milk

1/3 c. honey

½ c. brewed coffee

4 large eggs, beaten

1 c. walnuts chopped

1 tsp. of baking soda

Salt to taste

1 tsp. of baking powder

1 tsp. pure vanilla

½ tsp. cinnamon

Heat up your oven to 350 and prepare a pan for loaves with parchment paper. In a mixing bowl combine the flours, cinnamon, baking soda, of baking powder and salt. In another bowl beat the eggs, and mix with coconut oil, coconut milk and honey. Stir the egg mixture into the flour bowl and mix well. Once a smooth batter is made add in the walnuts. Pour into loaf pan. Bake30 minutes.

Pina Colada Bread

½ c. tapioca powder

½ c. sifted almond flour

½ c. coconut sugar

½ tsp. ground cinnamon

½ tsp. of baking soda

Salt to taste

2 ripe bananas

½ c. chopped pineapple

½ c. melted coconut oil

3 large eggs

1 tsp. pure vanilla extract

½ c. chopped pecans

Heat up the oven to 350 and line a bread loaf pan with parchment paper. In a mixing bowl, combine the flours, sugar, cinnamon, salt and baking soda. Then mix eggs, vanilla, oil, pineapple and bananas in a food processor until smooth. Stir into the flour bowl and mix well. Lastly, fold in the pecans. Pour into the bread pan and bake 45 minutes.

Flaxseed Bread

½ c. sifted coconut flour

1 ¼ c. sifted almond flour

¼ c. flax seeds ground

5 large eggs

Salt to taste

4 tbsp. melted coconut oil

1 tbsp. vinegar (apple cider)

Pinch. of baking soda

Heat up the oven to 350 degrees and grease a pan for loaves. Combine the flours, flaxseeds, salt and baking soda together in a mixing bowl. In another bowl mix the coconut oil, vinegar and whisked eggs together. Bake 45 minutes.

Irish Bread

2 ¾ c. sifted almond flour

¼ tsp. salt

1 ½ tsp. of baking soda

½ c. raisins

2 large whisked eggs

2 tbsp. honey

2 tbsp. vinegar (apple cider)

Heat the oven to 350 and line a baking sheet with parchment paper. Combine the flour, salt and baking soda well. In another bowl beat the eggs and mix in honey and vinegar. Then stir the egg mixture into the flour bowl. Work the mixture until a dough forms and roll it into a ball. Then flatten the ball out on the parchment paper. Make the circle 8 in. by 1 ½ in. Bake 20 minutes, turn off the oven and leave bread in warm oven for 10 minutes.

Banana and Blueberry Muffins

1 ¾ sifted almond flour

1 tsp. of baking soda

1/3 c. tapioca starch

2 tbsp. tapioca starch

¼ tsp. salt

½ tsp. cinnamon

1 tbsp. coconut oil

1 tbsp. apple juice

1 tsp. vanilla

½ c. banana

2 large eggs

2 c. blueberries

1/3 c. almonds (crushed slivers)

Heat up the oven to 375 and line a muffin pan with cupcake liners. Beat the eggs in a large mixing bowl, then mash the banana into it and add the rest of the ingredients except the blueberries and almonds. Once you have a smooth and fluffy batter add the blueberries and disperse throughout. Pour into muffin liners evenly and bake 15 minutes. Top with almond slivers.

Peach Muffins

1 c. sliced peaches

2 c. sifted almond flour

1 tsp. baking soda

1/8 tsp. salt

3 large eggs whisked

2 tbsp. melted butter

2 tbsp. melted honey

1 tbsp. lemon juice

Heat up the oven to 325 degrees and line a muffin pan with cupcake liners. In a mixing bowl combine the flour, baking soda and salt. In another bowl whisk the eggs and stir in melted butter and honey. Then add the lemon juice. Mix the egg mixture into the flour bowl and mix well. Lastly, stir in the peaches and pour into the cupcake liners evenly.

Zucchini Muffins

1 ½ almond flour (blanched)

2 tsp. cinnamon

1 tsp. nutmeg

½ tsp. salt

1 tsp. baking soda

3 large eggs whisked

¼ c. melted honey

1 tsp. pure vanilla

1 mashed banana

1 c. zucchini (remove skin and grate)

Heat up the oven to 350 and line a muffin pan with cupcake liners. Sift together all dry ingredients in a mixing bowl. In another bowl, beat the eggs and mash the banana. Mix the remaining wet ingredients and stir until light and fluffy. Then add zucchini and stir. Add the egg mixture into the flour mixture stirring rapidly. Divide between 12 muffin tins and bake 20 minutes.

Greek Yogurt Muffins

1 c. almond flour

1 c. brown rice

1 tbsp. of baking powder

½ tsp. of baking soda

½ tsp. salt

1 tbsp. cinnamon

1 tsp. ground cloves

1 tsp. nutmeg

2 large eggs whisked

1/3 c. applesauce (no added sugar)

1 1/3 c. Greek yogurt unsweetened

1 tbsp. vanilla

Melted honey

Cinnamon to taste

Heat up the oven to 375 and line a muffin tin with cupcake liners. In a large mixing bowl, combine flour, rice, of baking powder, baking soda, salt, cinnamon, cloves and nutmeg. Mix thoroughly. In another bowl, add the whisked eggs and stir in the Greek yogurt, vanilla and applesauce until smooth. Then stir the egg mixture into the flour mixture until smooth. Divide the batter between the cups, drizzle melted honey on them and sprinkle cinnamon on top.

Peanut Butter Muffins

1 ½ c. sifted almond flour

¼ c. whey protein

14 c. honey

2 ½ tsp. baking soda

Pinch of baking powder

Pinch of salt

4 oz. room temperature cream cheese (low fat)

½ c. creamy peanut butter

2 whisked eggs

1 c. unsweetened almond milk

2 tsp. pure vanilla

16 drops of stevia

Heat the oven to 350 and line a muffin tin with cupcake liners. In a medium bowl, combine the flour and dry ingredients well. Then blend the cream cheese, peanut butter and eggs until smooth. Then add in the vanilla extract and stevia. Beat this mixture into the flour bowl. Mix thoroughly (a hand mixer would be best) Add the milk and stir. When mixed completely, pour into muffin tins evenly and bake 25 minutes.

Snacks

Multi Nut & Seed Crackers

½ c. almond flour (blanched)

½ c. macadamia nuts

1 tbsp. coconut flour

¼ c. pumpkin seeds

2 tbsp. sesame seeds

2 tbsp. hemp seeds

1 tbsp. flax meal

Salt to taste

¼ c. water

1 tbsp. room temperature butter

Heat oven up to 300 and prepare a piece of parchment paper on a baking sheet. Process the macadamia nuts in the food processor until fine. Add in the flours, seeds, salt and flax meal. Pulse until ground with little chunks. Then add in butter and water to form the dough. Roll the dough into a ball and sprinkle with coconut flour. Using a rolling pin, roll the dough out on the parchment paper into a huge rectangle that is ¼ inch thick. Cut 25 2x2 squares into the dough. Bake 23 minutes.

Graham Crackers

1 ½ c. almond flour (blanched)

1 tbsp. arrowroot powder

¼ tsp. salt

Cinnamon to taste

2 tbsp. melted honey

Heat up the oven to 350 and line a baking sheet with parchment paper. Sift together the flour, powder, salt and cinnamon. Then add to the food processor with the honey and syrup. Roll a ball of dough and place on the parchment paper. Using a rolling pin, roll it out into a ¼ of an inch thick rectangle. Cut into 5 by 2.5 inch rectangles. Draw the typical graham cracker design on each rectangle by drawing a line down the middle width wise and length wise and poke holes. Bake 8 minutes then cool

Fig Crackers

1 ½ c. almond flour (blanched)

½ tsp. salt

1 tsp. rosemary

4 figs (dried and chopped)

1 whisked egg

1 tbsp. olive oil

Heat up the oven to 350 and line a baking sheet with parchment paper. Combine all ingredients in the food processor. Add the egg last. Pulse until a smooth dough is formed. Roll it into a ball and place it on the parchment paper. Then using a rolling pin, roll it into a ½ of an inch thick square. Cut into 2 by 2 inch squares and bake for 10 minutes.

Peanut Butter Granola Bars

½ c. peanut butter

¼ c. maple syrup

1 egg

¼ tsp. salt

1 c. almond flour (blanched

½ c. walnuts

¼ c. almonds (sliced)

¼ c. sunflower seeds

¼ c. chocolate chips (miniature)

¼ c. ground flax seed

1 tbsp. chia seeds

1 tbsp. sesame seeds

Heat up the oven to 350 and grease a square 8 inch baking pan. Mix together the peanut butter, salt, honey and egg and beat until smooth. Add the nuts into the food processor and chop them. Then mix them in a new bowl with the flour, chocolate, flax, chia and sesame seeds. Combine the two bowls together until smooth. Transfer into the baking pan and press into the bottom. Bake 20 minutes then cool and cut into rectangles.

Cranberry Chocolate Power Bars

1 c. almond flour (blanched)

1 tbsp. sifted coconut flour

2 tbsp. flax meal (ground)

Salt to taste

½ tsp. baking soda

2 tbsp. coconut sugar

2 large eggs

½ c. dried cranberries

1/3 c. dark chocolate chips

Heat the oven to 350 degrees and grease an 8 inch square baking dish. Mix the flours, meal baking soda and salt together. Then add in the sugar and eggs and mix rapidly for a few minutes until smooth. Add in the cranberries and dark chocolate chips and mix well. Press into the baking dish and bake for 15 minutes. Cut into rectangles and enjoy. Save extras in an air tight container in the fridge.

White Chocolate and Macadamia Nut Bars

1 c. almond flour (blanched)

½ c. macadamia nuts (chopped)

1/3 c. white chocolate (chopped)

¼ c. ground flax seed

¼ c. coconut flakes (unsweetened)

2 tbsp. chia seeds

½ c. almond butter (no salt)

¼ c. maple syrup

1 tbsp. vanilla

1 whisked egg

¼ tsp. salt

Heat up your oven to 350 and grease an 8 by 8 inch baking dish. In a large mixing bowl combine the flour, nuts, chocolate, flax, chia seeds and coconut. In another bowl beat the egg and then stir in the butter, syrup, vanilla and salt. Mix well then pour into the flour bowl. Mix the dough thoroughly then press into the baking dish evenly. Bake 20 minutes, cool and cut into rectangle snack bars.

Almond Joy Bars

½ c. almond flour

½ c. sifted coconut flour

¾ c. coconut sugar

2 tsp. almond extract

¾ c. full fat coconut milk

4 whisked eggs

¼ tsp. salt

1/3 tsp. baking soda

¼ c. coconut (shredded and unsweetened)

¾ c. chocolate chips

Heat up the oven to 350 and grease an 8 inch square pan. In a mixing bowl, combine the eggs, milk, extract and sugar. In another bowl mix the flours, salt and baking soda. Combine the two mixtures together until smooth. Pour into the baking dish. Top with coconut and chocolate chips. Bake 30 minutes. Cool and cut into bars.

Nacho Cheese Bread

2 c. almond flour (blanched)

8 oz. cheddar cheese (shredded)

1 large egg

1 tsp. salt

1 tsp. baking soda

1 tsp. chili powder

Heat up the oven to 375 and line a baking sheet with parchment paper. In a mixing bowl sift together the dry ingredients and cheese. In another bowl, whisk the egg and then add into the dry ingredients and thoroughly combine. Roll the dough into a ball, then flatten it out with a rolling pin into a flat circle that is about 2/3 of an inch thick. Bake 10 minutes. Great with dipping sauce.

Cranberry Biscotti

3 c. almond flour (blanched)

2 whisked eggs

½ c. honey

½ c. cranberries (dried)

½ tsp. baking soda

¼ tsp. salt

1 tbsp. vanilla

½ c. pecans (chopped)

Heat up the oven to 325 degrees and line a baking sheet with parchment paper. In a mixing bowl rapidly mix the eggs, honey and vanilla for 5 minutes. Separately, sift the flour, baking soda and salt together. Mix the egg mixture into the dry bowl and beat well. Fold in pecans and cranberries. Roll the dough into a log 1 foot long by 3 inches. Bake for 30 minutes. Cool and slice into ½ in. slices then bake for 30 more minutes. Flip the biscotti after the first 15 minutes.

Desserts

Apple Crisp Crumble

½ c. almond flour (blanched)

8 c. sliced apples (skins and cores removed)

2 tbsp. flax meal (brown)

¼ tsp. salt

1 tbsp. ground cinnamon

1 tbsp. ginger (ground)

2 tbsp. shortening

2 tbsp. raw honey

1 tbsp. vanilla

½ c. pecans (processed)

Heat up the oven to 350 and grease a 2 qt. dish. Mix together the flour, flax meal, spices and salt until well combined. The beat in the shortening, vanilla and melted honey. Work through it so a dough forms. Add in the chopped pecans and disperse throughout the dough, Place apples in the bottom of baking dish and crumble the dough on top of them. Cover. Bake 70 minutes. Uncover, brown the top of the crumble.

Peach Crisp

6 sliced peaches

1 tbsp. lemon juice

1 tbsp. pure vanilla extract

1 ½ c. almond flour (blanched)

3 tbsp. arrowroot powder

½ tsp. salt

1/3 c. grape seed oil

¼ c. melted honey

Heat up the oven to 350 and grease a 2 quart baking pan. In a large mixing bowl, combine the peaches, vanilla, lemon juice and arrow root powder together well. In another bowl add the flour, baking soda, salt, melted honey and grape seed oil. Mix well until crumble forms. Pour the peach bowl into the baking dish and spread the crumbles over the top. Cover with foil and bake for 1 hour. Remove the foil afterward and bake until the top browns.

Chocolate Covered Butter Cookies

2 c. almond flour (blanched)

½ c. sun butter

2 tbsp. butter

¼ tsp. salt

1 tsp. baking soda

2 tbsp. honey

1 tbsp. vanilla

1 c. dark chocolate chips

Heat up the oven to 350 and line a baking sheet with a piece of parchment paper. Have another piece of parchment paper on hand. In a medium bowl, mix the flour, baking soda and salt thoroughly. Transfer to a food processor and add in butter, vanilla and honey. Make a smooth dough and roll it out to ¼ inch thick. Place in the freezer 15 minutes, Cut out 2 inch circles using a cookie cutter, lather each of them with a spread of sun butter. Bake 5 minutes then let cool for about an hour. Place back in the freezer 10 minutes. Then heat a small saucepan over low heat and melt the chocolate. Dip each cookie in the chocolate then place on parchment paper and freeze again until set.

Honey Butter Cookies

2 ½ c. almond flour (blanched)

½ tsp. salt

½ c. room temperature butter (salted)

¼ c. honey

1 tbsp. vanilla

Heat the oven to 350 and line a baking dish with parchment paper. In a small mixing bowl sift together the flour and salt. Mix in butter, honey and vanilla until the dough becomes smooth. Divide the dough into two balls and roll it out using a rolling pin. The flat ball should be about ½ inch tall. Freeze for 30 minutes then cut out cookies using your favorite cookie cutter. Bake 6 minutes.

PB & J Cookies

1 ¼ c. almond flour (blanched)

½ c. peanut butter (smooth)

¼ c. shortening (vegan)

½ c. coconut sugar

1 large egg (whisked)

½ tsp. salt

½ c. raspberry jam

Heat up the oven to 350 and line a baking sheet with parchment paper. Using a food processor or hand blender combine the peanut butter, sugar, shortening and egg and mix until a creamy smooth texture is made. Then add is the flour and mix until no lumps remain. Then add the salt. Scoop the dough out by the table spoon and flatten into a circle on the parchment paper. Make a little indention in the middle of each cookie for the raspberry jam. Bake 10 minutes.

Peanut Butter Cookies

1 c. almond flour (blanched)

1/3 tsp. salt

¼ tsp. baking soda

1/3 c. peanut butter

¼ c. honey

2 tbsp. shortening

1 tsp. pure vanilla

Heat up the oven to 350 and line a baking sheet with parchment paper. Sift together the dry ingredients until well combined. In a food processor combine the peanut butter, honey, vanilla and shortening until smooth. Add the flour in and pulse until well combined. Spoon out 1 tbsp. at a time and roll into balls. Flatten them on the parchment paper and bake 8 minutes until light brown.

Pumpkin Pie Bars

1 c. almond flour (blanched)

2 whisked eggs

½ c. honey

½ c. pureed pumpkin

Pinch of salt

1/3 tsp. baking soda

Pinch of cinnamon

¼ tsp. nutmeg

¼ tsp. ground cloves

Heat the oven up to 350 degrees and grease an 8 inch square baking dish. In a medium mixing bowl, whisk the eggs until frothy and mix the pumpkin and honey until smooth. In another bowl sift together all the dry ingredients. Mix the pumpkin mixture into the flour mixture. When smooth, pour into the pan and bake 30 minutes. Top with whipped cream and a sprinkle of cinnamon.

Coconut Pie Bars

½ c. almond flour (blanched)

1 tbsp. coconut flour

3 whisked eggs

1 c. coconut milk

½ c. melted coconut oil

½ c. honey

1 tbsp. vanilla

1 ½ c. coconut (shredded and not sweetened)

Pinch of Salt

Heat up the oven to 350 and grease an 8 inch square dish. Combine the whisked eggs with melted coconut oil, melted honey and vanilla. Mix until fluffy. In another bowl sift together the flours, coconut and salt. Mix the two together then pour into a baking dish. Bake 30 minutes, refrigerate and serve cold.

Mocha Latte Bars

½ c. almond flour (blanched)

2 tbsp. sifted coconut flour

¼ c. butter

1 ½ tsp. espresso beans (ground)

4 whisked eggs

1 c. coconut sugar

1 tbsp. vanilla

1 c. chocolate pieces

¼ tsp. salt

Heat up the oven to 350 and grease an 8 inch square dish. In a small saucepan add the chocolate and carefully melt (it will easily burn). Add the butter in and melt. Then add in the ground beans and take the pan off the heat. In a food processor add the eggs, sugar, salt and vanilla until fluffy. Then add in the flours and mix well. Add the chocolate mixture into the rest of the ingredients and mix thoroughly. Pour into greased pan and bake 25 minutes. Slice and serve.

Made in the USA
Las Vegas, NV
14 February 2024

85749468R00024